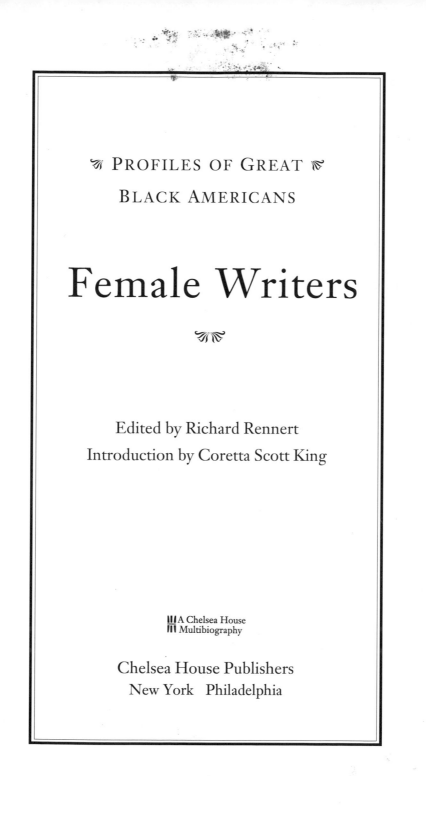

&#x7f;❧ PROFILES OF GREAT ❧&#x7f;
BLACK AMERICANS

# Female Writers

❧❧

Edited by Richard Rennert
Introduction by Coretta Scott King

⫴ A Chelsea House
⫴ Multibiography

Chelsea House Publishers
New York   Philadelphia

Copyright © 1994 by Chelsea House Publishers, a division of
Main Line Book Co. All rights reserved. Printed and bound in the
United States of America.

First Printing

1  3  5  7  9  8  6  4  2

Library of Congress Cataloging-in-Publication Data

  Female writers/edited by Richard Rennert; introduction by
Coretta Scott King.
    p. cm.—(Profiles of great black Americans)
  Includes bibliographical references and index.
  Summary: A collection of short biographies of noted black female
writers, including Maya Angelou, Gwendolyn Brooks, and Nikki
Giovanni.
    ISBN    0-7910-2063-0.
              0-7910-2064-9 (pbk.)
        1. Afro-American women authors—Biography—Juvenile
literature. [1. Authors, American. 2. Afro-Americans—Biography.]
I. Rennert, Richard Scott, 1956–   . II. Series.
93-21673                                          PS153.N5F46 1994
810.9'9287—dc20                                            CIP
  [B]                                                        AC

# ❧ CONTENTS ❧

## by Coretta Scott King

This book is about black Americans who served society through the excellence of their achievements. It forms a part of the rich history of black men and women in America—a history of stunning accomplishments in every field of human endeavor, from literature and art to science, industry, education, diplomacy, athletics, jurisprudence, even polar exploration.

Not all of the people in this history had the same ideals, but I think you will find something that all of them had in common. Like Martin Luther King, Jr., they all decided to become "drum majors" and serve humanity. In that principle—whether it was expressed in books, inventions, or song—they found something outside themselves to use as a goal and a guide. Something that showed them a way to serve others instead of only living for themselves.

Reading the stories of these courageous men and women not only helps us discover the principles that we will use to guide our own lives but also teaches us about our black heritage and about America itself. It is crucial for us to know the heroes and heroines of our history and to realize that the price we paid in our struggle for equality in America was dear. But we must also understand that we have gotten as far as we have partly because America's democratic system and ideals made it possible.

We are still struggling with racism and prejudice. But the great men and women in this series are a tribute to the spirit of our democratic ideals and the system in which they have flourished. And that makes their stories special and worth knowing.

MAYA ANGELOU

A multitalented artist and one of the most remarkable personalities on the American scene, Maya Angelou was born Marguerite Johnson on April 4, 1928, in St. Louis, Missouri. Her parents, Bailey and Vivian Baxter Johnson, divorced when Marguerite was only three years old. At that time, she and her four-year-old brother, Bailey, Jr., were sent to live with their paternal grandmother in

Stamps, Arkansas. Annie "Momma" Henderson, the children's grandmother, made a meager living from her small-town general store, but she provided her grandchildren with a warm and loving home. She taught them self-reliance, courage, and faith and gave them the sense that nothing was beyond their ability to achieve if they wanted it enough.

When Marguerite was seven, her life took a strange and terrible detour. During a visit with her mother in St. Louis, she was raped by her mother's boyfriend. The man was convicted of the crime and, according to Angelou, was murdered for his misdeeds before he could begin serving his sentence. Believing that she was somehow responsible for the man's death, Marguerite retreated into silence and did not speak for five years.

Back in her grandmother's house, the young girl found the understanding and support that she needed during her painful withdrawal. "Sister, Mama don't care what these people say about you," her grandmother told her. "Mama know, Sister, when you and the good Lord get ready, you're gonna be a preacher." Marguerite also found an older friend, Mrs. Bertha Flowers, who refused to write her off. Rather than comparing her to other children, Mrs. Flowers treated Marguerite as an individual with her own needs and talents. After five years, the young girl was finally able to emerge from her self-imposed silence. By the time she was finished with the eighth grade, she ranked at the head of her class.

At this point, Marguerite was reunited with her mother in San Francisco, where Vivian was operating a boardinghouse. The atmosphere was quite different from the one she had known in Arkansas. Her mother associated with a sophisticated and fast-living crowd, and Marguerite was soon caught up in her world. She became pregnant and at the age of 16 gave birth to a son, Guy. She later called this event "the best thing that ever happened to me."

Motherhood at such a young age might have led Marguerite to become more dependent on her own mother, but instead it inspired her to make a life for herself and her baby. The road was far from easy. She worked as a cook and a waitress, and even delved into the world of prostitution as a small-time madam. At the age of 22, she married a white man named Tosh Angelos. The marriage ended two and a half years later, but Marguerite came out of it with more life experience and a new identity—Maya Angelou.

Angelou had taken dance lessons while in high school, and now she determined to exploit her talent. She began by performing in a succession of Los Angeles bars and eventually worked her way up to the better night spots. Her career took a major step forward in 1954, when she was chosen to take part in an overseas tour of George and Ira Gershwin's classic musical *Porgy and Bess.*

When she returned from the tour, Angelou was no longer content to be merely a performer. She had developed a keen social awareness, and she was in-

spired by the work of Dr. Martin Luther King, Jr.,
who was leading the movement for black civil rights
in the South. At King's request, Angelou spent two
years in the North seeking support for the civil rights
movement. "We are all diminished when one group is
diminished," she later reflected. "Can you imagine if
this country were not so afflicted with racism? Can
you imagine what it would be like if the vitality,
humor, and resilience of the black American were
infused throughout this country?"

Angelou certainly saw to it that her own best
qualities came to the fore. Her work as an activist
brought her into contact with some of the leading
African American writers of the day, including James
Baldwin and Paule Marshall, and she developed the
desire to become a writer as well.

It was not Angelou's way to shut herself in a room
with a typewriter. Instead, she set off boldly for Africa
with her son and a South African freedom fighter
named Vusumzi Make. The three settled in Cairo,
Egypt, where Angelou took a job as an editor with a
newspaper entitled the *Arab Observer*. However, Make
resented Angelou's desire for a career of her own, and
the couple eventually split up. Angelou and her son
then went to live in the West African nation of Ghana,
where Angelou found steady employment as both a
journalist and a teacher.

By the mid-1960s, Angelou decided that her true
home was the United States. When she returned, her
career exploded in a breathtaking number of direc-
tions. She began to both write plays and act in them,

and in 1971, when she wrote the script for the film *Georgia, Georgia*, she became the first black woman to have a screenplay produced.

The achievement that brought Angelou national attention was the 1970 publication of *I Know Why the Caged Bird Sings*, an account of her life up to the birth of her son. Nominated for the prestigious National Book Award, the book was followed by four more volumes of autobiography: *Gather Together in My Name* (1974), *Singin' and Swingin' and Gettin' Merry Like Christmas* (1976), *The Heart of a Woman* (1981), and *All God's Children Need Traveling Shoes* (1986).

"I don't tell everything I know," Angelou said of her autobiography, "but what I do tell is the truth. There's a world of difference between truth and facts. Facts can obscure the truth. You can tell so many facts that you fill the stage but haven't got one iota of the truth."

Angelou also became well known to television viewers because of her role in the 1977 production of *Roots*, Alex Haley's saga of his family's history from its African origins through the days of slavery. Angelou's performance in the ground-breaking miniseries earned her a nomination for an Emmy Award. In 1979, *I Know Why the Caged Bird Sings* was adapted into a television movie, for which Angelou not only wrote the script but also composed the sound track.

As her artistic career flourished, Angelou continued to concern herself with social issues. In recognition of her growing stature, President Gerald Ford appointed her to the commission charged with coordinating the celebration of the U.S. bicentennial in 1976. Two years later, President Jimmy Carter named her as a member of the Commission of International Woman's Year, which culminated in a major conference sponsored by the United Nations in Nairobi, Kenya.

Angelou's intellectual achievements were signally honored in 1981, when Wake Forest University, in Winston-Salem, North Carolina, granted her a lifetime appointment as Reynolds Professor of American Studies. In addition to continuing her autobiography with such volumes as *The Heart of a Woman*, Angelou devoted much of her energy to poetry and published several verse collections, including *Just Give Me a Cool Drink of Water 'fore I Diiie*, *And Still I Rise*, and *I Shall Not Be Moved*.

With the conservative administrations of Ronald Reagan and George Bush holding power in Washington, the 1980s were not an enjoyable decade politically for the outspoken and progressive Angelou. With the election of Bill Clinton to the presidency in 1992, however, Angelou emerged with more stature than ever. At President Clinton's inauguration ceremony on January 20, 1993, Angelou was chosen to read her poem "On the Pulse of Morning" on the steps of the Capitol just before the new president took his oath of office. It was an event that thrilled her many fans and brought her squarely back into the public eye.

Shortly after the inauguration, Angelou was appointed chairwoman of the annual Horatio Alger

Award dinner in the nation's capital. She herself had been a 1992 recipient of the award, which honors individuals who have overcome adversity to become major achievers. Angelou declared that she was "bowled over by the honor" of organizing the prestigious dinner but also acted swiftly to put her own mark on what was traditionally a sedate and formal social function. Under her supervision, the dinner was enlivened by strolling musicians playing a wide variety of music, and the menu was changed to include some of Angelou's favorite southern dishes.

Throughout her extraordinary and adventurous life, Angelou has drawn strength from her unquenchable optimism, a quality she offered to the entire nation in the conclusion of her inauguration poem:

*Here on the pulse of this new day*
*You may have the grace to look up and out*
*And into your sister's eyes, into*
*Your brother's face, your country*
*And say simply*
*Very simply*
*With hope*
*Good morning.*

GWENDOLYN BROOKS

The first black American writer to win a Pulitzer Prize, Gwendolyn Brooks was born in Topeka, Kansas, on June 7, 1917. Her parents, David Anderson Brooks and Keziah Corinne Wims Brooks, provided her with a loving and stimulating home life.

Young Gwendolyn began writing when she was seven. By the age of 11, she was collecting her poems in composition books. Her parents, convinced that she had an exceptional talent, encouraged her to believe that anything was possible.

By the time she was 15, Brooks was boldly sending her manuscripts to well-known writers. Among them was James Weldon Johnson, the eminent poet, novelist, diplomat, educator, and civil rights leader. Then a professor of literature at Fisk University in Nashville, Tennessee, Johnson took the trouble to send the manuscripts back with comments and suggestions. "He thought I was talented and hoped that I would keep writing," Brooks later recalled. "My parents were delighted with all of this attention. . . . But I would have gone on writing. I didn't care what any of them said."

Though her mother had gone home to Topeka to give birth to her, Brooks grew up in the city of Chicago. When she attended high school, she was surrounded by large numbers of whites for the first time and found the experience disturbing. Accustomed to attention and support in her early years, Brooks now found that she was shunted to the side. She observed that society was divided along racial lines; rather than creating a desire to be accepted by the dominant group, the experience taught her to value her own personality and racial identity. Concentrating on her studies, she became a keen student of literature and delved into the work of all the leading modern poets.

After graduating from high school, Brooks enrolled in Woodrow Wilson Junior College. In 1938, when she was 21, she met Henry Lowington Blakely II and married him shortly afterward. The couple separated briefly at the end of the 1960s, but in 1989 they celebrated their 50th wedding anniversary.

Nothing in Brooks's life was more important to her than her poetry. "In writing poetry you're interested in condensation so you don't try to put all of a particular impression or inspiration on a single page. You distill. Poetry is life distilled."

In 1941, her writing received a major stimulus when she attended a poetry workshop in Chicago's South Side Community Art Center and shared her work and ideas with other writers. Two years later, her work earned her a prize from the Midwestern Writers' Conference. When in 1945 the prestigious firm of Harper & Brothers published her first collection of poems, *A Street in Bronzeville*, her career was definitely launched. Critics were deeply impressed by this young poet who had mastered all the complicated techniques of modern poetry but firmly focused her gaze on the trials and tribulations of her people. Distinguished African American writers of the earlier generation, such as Claude McKay and Countee Cullen, and those of her own generation, such as Ralph Ellison and Richard Wright, enthusiastically welcomed Brooks into their ranks.

With the success of her first book, many doors opened to Brooks. In 1946 and 1947, her work was aided by Guggenheim Fellowships, and she also received financial support from the nation's most prestigious cultural associations, the American

Academy of Arts and Letters and the National Institute of Arts and Letters.

Brooks's second book of poems, *Annie Allen,* was published in 1949 and more than justified the support she had been given. The following year, the book was awarded the Pulitzer Prize. Never before had a black American captured this coveted award.

The Pulitzer spurred an outpouring of work from Brooks. In 1953, she published an autobiographical novel, *Maud Martha,* which was not a record of her life but a distillation of her experience. "I didn't want to write about somebody who turned out to be a star," she explained, "'cause most people don't turn out to be stars. And yet their lives are just as sweet and just as rich as any others and often they are richer and sweeter." Critics later recognized that *Maud Martha* was ahead of its time in its exploration of feminist themes, an approach that was not widely understood until the growth of the women's movement in the late 1960s.

In 1956, Brooks published her first book of children's poems, *Bronzeville Boys and Girls.* She followed in 1960 with another adult verse collection, *The Bean Eaters. The Bean Eaters* took a critical view of race relations in America: Among other topics, Brooks's poems dealt with the 1957 school desegregation battle in Little Rock, Arkansas, and the brutal lynching of Emmett Till, a black teenager, in Mississippi in 1955.

In 1968, Brooks made a literary breakthrough with *In the Mecca,* a book that had started out as a novel and ended as a long narrative poem interspersed with ballads. *In the Mecca* recounts a mother's search for her lost child in the Mecca Building in Chicago; the search becomes a rogues' gallery of the people who inhabit the run-down building and exposes the failure of their lives and of the society in which they live. Nevertheless, the poem also carries a positive message.

> *Build with lithe love. With love like lion-eyes.*
> *With love like morningrise.*
> *With love like black, our black.*

Despite the fact that her work was gaining widespread acceptance—*In the Mecca* was favorably reviewed and nominated for a National Book Award, and Brooks was named poet laureate of the state of Illinois—Brooks grew increasingly disenchanted with the white literary establishment. In 1969, she announced that she was leaving Harper & Row and would henceforth deal only with black publishers. Her reason for this, she said, was to "clarify my language. I want these poems to be free. I want them to be direct without sacrificing the kinds of music, the picturemaking I've always been interested in." Changing to black publishers was a way of reaching out to a larger audience of black readers. Her next book of poems, *Riot*, as well as a number of later volumes, were published by Broadside, a Detroit firm run by the prominent black poet Dudley Randall. Later, in 1987, Brooks founded her own press, the David Company.

*Riot* also marked a change in Brooks's style, as the literary tone of her earlier work gave way to more direct language accessible to the average reader. This was a result of Brooks's decision to focus on the black community—she had abandoned her earlier belief in integration and was now convinced that African Americans needed to build their own institutions. She began to sponsor poetry contests for young  people and to conduct poetry workshops, one of  which involved a powerful Chicago youth gang known as the Blackstone Rangers. The experience was rejuvenating for Brooks, who later recalled: "The young people that I met in the late sixties . . . educated me. They gave me books to read. We talked and talked. They just absorbed me, adopted me." Brooks also began to spend a good deal of time working with prison inmates, reading them her poems and encouraging them to write.

Following *Riot*, Brooks continued to write prolifically, producing such volumes as *Aloneness, Broadside Treasury, Jump Bad, Beckonings*, and a straightforward autobiography, *Report from Part One*. By the 1980s, her stature as one of America's leading poets was firmly established. In 1989, Brooks's many admirers held a public celebration of her 70th birthday at Navy Pier in Chicago, and the National Endowment for the Arts awarded her a $48,000 Lifetime Achievement Award. In 1990, Chicago State University created a Gwendolyn Brooks Distinguished Chair of Creative Writing and appropriately chose Brooks herself to fill the post.

Brooks made it clear that this new wave of acceptance would not change her attitude or diminish her independence. "There are so many blacks who are denying all blackness. They think they can twinkle their fingers at blackness and it'll just go away and they'll be loved by whites and accepted." She often reiterated her admiration for the assassinated civil rights leader Malcolm X, who, she said, "believed black people should love black people and value them above all others." Even in her seventies, she was still the same fearless poet who had written back in 1949: "First fight. Then fiddle."

NIKKI GIOVANNI

A challenging poet with a powerful social message, Yolande Cornelia "Nikki" Giovanni was born in Knoxville, Tennessee, on June 7, 1943. When Nikki and her older sister, Gary, were still very young, the family moved to Cincinnati, Ohio. Nikki's father, Jones "Gus" Giovanni, worked as a probation officer, and her mother, Yolande Watson Giovanni, was a social worker. When she was

14, Nikki moved back to Knoxville to attend high school, living with her maternal grandparents, John and Louvenia Watson. Originally from Georgia, Louvenia Watson had spoken out so strongly against southern racism that her family had finally smuggled her out of town for her own safety. Her strong-willed, independent nature exerted a powerful and lasting influence on Nikki: even as a youngster, she often stuck up for her older sister.

Giovanni was an excellent student at Knoxville's Austin High School, and at the age of 17 she entered Fisk University in Nashville. However, when she decided to go back to Knoxville for Thanksgiving without asking permission, she came into conflict with the dean of women, who promptly suspended her. Refusing to give in, Giovanni went back to Cincinnati and lived with her parents for the next several years. During that time, she worked in a drugstore, assumed full-time care of her nephew Christopher, and took some courses at the University of Cincinnati. She finally returned to Fisk in 1964, when the university appointed a new dean, Blanche M. Cowan, who became both a friend and a mentor to Giovanni. This time she adapted eagerly to college life and graduated magna cum laude in 1967.

While at Fisk, Giovanni took part in the Fisk Writers Workshop, which was directed by John Oliver Killens, a noted black author with strong opinions about racial and political issues. Giovanni, having grown up in a middle-class professional family, had entered college in 1960 as a conservative Republican.

Responding to the ideas of Killens and to the political upheavals of the late 1960s, she emerged from Fisk as a socially conscious writer and a progressive activist. She was a charter member of the Student Nonviolent Coordinating Committee (SNCC) and organized the Black Arts Festival in Cincinnati. Her first book of poems, *Black Feeling, Black Talk*, published in 1967, took an angry and militant view of race relations in the United States. Some readers were shocked and disturbed by her call for African Americans to combat racism by violent means. However, this was an attitude shared by other young black writers who had grown up during the nonviolent phase of the civil rights movement and saw little real change in American society.

Under a certain amount of pressure from her parents, Giovanni decided to continue her education. With a grant from the Ford Foundation, she enrolled in the University of Pennsylvania School of Social Work. But she soon realized that her true interest was in literature and enrolled in the School of Fine Arts at Columbia University in New York. Though she left Columbia before completing her master of fine arts degree, she was appointed assistant professor of English at Queens College, teaching in the socially progressive SEEK program. During this time, her poetry began to shift away from purely political themes. Her second volume of poems, *Black Judgment*, mixed political concerns with personal issues: the poem entitled "Nikki-Rosa," a tough-minded celebration of childhood memories, emerged as one of her most popular works and has been included in many anthologies:

> *I really hope no white person ever has cause*
> *to write about me*
> *because they never understand*
> *Black love is Black wealth and they'll*
> *probably talk about my hard childhood*
> *and never understand that*
> *all the while I was quite happy.*

During the 1970s, Giovanni's poetry became more spiritual and inward looking. The volumes of poetry she published during the decade—*Re-Creation* (1970), *My House* (1972), *The Women and the Men* (1972), and *Cotton Candy on a Rainy Day* (1978)—do not ignore politics but concern themselves principally with personal relationships. One of the factors in this evolution was the birth of Giovanni's son, Thomas Watson, in 1969. In keeping with her frank and independent personality, Giovanni made it clear in public statements that she had made a conscious choice to have a child without being married.

If motherhood altered Giovanni's approach to writing, it also broadened her range of activities. Long concerned with the self-image developed by black children, Giovanni decided to establish her own publishing company, NikTom, in 1970. She herself wrote three volumes of children's poetry: *Spin a Soft Black Song* (1971), *Ego-Tripping and Other Poems for Young Readers* (1973), and *Vacation Time: Poems for*

*Children* (1980). One of her principal themes in these poems is the celebration of African roots. In the poem "Ego-Tripping," for example, she evokes the power of African mythology:

> *I was born in the congo*
> *I walked to the fertile crescent and built*
> *the sphinx*
> *I designed a pyramid so tough that a star*
> *that only glows every one hundred years falls*
> *into the center giving divine perfect light*
> *I am bad.*

Though she is best known as a poet, Giovanni's career has many other facets. In 1971, she published her first collection of essays, *Gemini: An Extended Autobiographical Statement on My First Twenty-five Years of Being a Black Poet.* In *Gemini*, she explored the roots of her art, ranging from childhood to the birth of her son. The book impressed readers with its freshness and honesty and was nominated for a National Book Award.

Having both studied and taught literature, Giovanni was always keenly aware of the debt she owed to African American writers of earlier generations. In *A Dialogue: James Baldwin and Nikki Giovanni* (1973) and *A Poetic Equation: Conversations Between Nikki Giovanni and Margaret Walker* (1974), she paid tribute to two of the writers who had most influenced her. At the same time, these books were a valuable study of the changes in thinking and literary technique from one generation of African American writers to another.

Quite early in her career, Giovanni discovered that she had a flair for reading her own work and always relished direct interaction with her audiences. Between 1975 and 1978, for example, she made no fewer than 200 personal appearances. Like many other poets, she also understood the close relationship between poetry and music. In 1972, she made her first record album, *Truth Is on Its Way*, in which she read her poems to a background of gospel music. The success of the album led to several more, including *Like a Ripple on a Pond*, *The Way I Feel*, and *The Reason I Like Chocolate*.

During the 1980s and early 1990s, Giovanni's writing shifted back to larger concerns. Unlike her more racially militant approach during the 1960s, her outlook this time focused more on humanity as a whole and the problems common to all peoples. Her independence often caused controversy: in 1984, she refused to endorse a boycott of the white supremacist regime in South Africa, declaring that "a nation 80 percent black cannot be treated as if it were a soft drink or the grocery store on the corner." Her position on this issue drew much criticism from American blacks and even resulted in death threats.

Giovanni's contributions to literature have been increasingly recognized by the academic community. In addition to receiving honorary doctorates from Fisk and Indiana universities, she served as a visiting professor at Ohio State University and at the College of Mount St. Joseph, and in 1989 she took up a permanent faculty position at Virginia Polytechnic Institute.

Throughout her career, Giovanni's versatility led some critics to complain that her writing was not as polished as it ought to be. She responded by admitting that she was not the kind of writer who could confine herself to a room with the idea of producing a perfect work of art: "I like the story and I care more about *what* is being said than about *how* it is said." Giovanni is above all a communicator, and in this role she will continue to be a vibrant influence in American culture:

> *and if ever i touched a life i hope that life knows*
> *that I know that touching was and still is and*
> *always will be the true*
> *revolution.*

LORRAINE HANSBERRY

O ne of the outstanding play-
wrights in the history of the American theater,
Lorraine Vivian Hansberry was born in Chicago,
Illinois, on May 19, 1930. The youngest of four
children, she was raised in a prosperous and cultivated
environment. Her father, Carl Augustus Hansberry,
was a successful real estate broker who was active in
the Republican party and in civil rights organizations;

her mother, Nannie Perry Hansberry, was a school-teacher and a leader in Chicago's political and cultural life. Adding additional luster to the family, one of Lorraine's uncles, Leo Hansberry, was a professor of African history at Howard University in Washington, D.C.

The Hansberrys enjoyed a prominent position in Chicago's black community and often entertained visiting dignitaries. While growing up, Lorraine met such African American celebrities as the actor Paul Robeson, the composer Duke Ellington, heavyweight boxing champion Joe Louis, and Olympic track star Jesse Owens. She also grew up with an awareness of racism, because her parents actively opposed Chicago's unofficial system of segregated housing, which had created a crowded black ghetto on the city's South Side.

Despite the Hansberrys' affluence, Lorraine attended Chicago's public schools, graduating from Englewood High School in 1947. Her parents were both graduates of all-black colleges in the South and wanted her to enroll at Howard. But Hansberry showed her independence by choosing the University of Wisconsin at Madison, where the vast majority of students were white—indeed, she was the first black student to live in her freshman dormitory. Left-wing political views held sway at the Madison campus, and Hansberry involved herself in such causes as the Young Progressive League and the 1948 presidential campaign of third-party candidate Henry Wallace. She also discovered the power of the drama to convey a social message in poetic form when she saw a production of the Irish author Sean O'Casey's *Juno and the Paycock*. Later on, she was to recapture O'Casey's deep feeling for his native culture in her own portrayal of African American life in Chicago.

After two years at Madison, Hansberry began to find college life too far removed from the political realities that concerned her. She dropped out and moved to New York City, where she went to work for Paul Robeson's radical newspaper, *Freedom*. Writing about politics while also reviewing books and plays, she was promoted to associate editor in 1952. Meanwhile, the experience of living in Harlem, New York's leading black community, stimulated her creative impulses, and she began to produce plays and short stories. Before long, writing would become her main interest.

Before launching her literary career, Hansberry married Robert Nemiroff, a white college student who was an aspiring poet and songwriter. The young couple decided to devote themselves to writing, working at odd jobs to make ends meet. In 1953, Hansberry quit her newspaper job and began to work seriously on three plays that were in the early stages of development. During that time, she made a living by working as a typist, a garment worker, and a camp director.

When Nemiroff and a friend wrote a hit song, Hansberry was able to stop working and write full time. Her efforts now focused on a play she first entitled *The Crystal Stair*, which concerned the struggles of a black family on Chicago's South Side. When she finished the play in 1957, Hansberry read it to a number of friends, and they were deeply impressed by its power and originality. Phil Rose, a music publisher who had worked with Nemiroff, tried to interest Broadway producers in the play, but he could not find anyone willing to take a chance on a serious drama that presented black people as complex, rounded human beings. Rose decided to produce the play himself in association with a group of backers. After a series of successful trial runs in New Haven, Philadelphia, and Chicago, Hansberry's play, now entitled *A Raisin in the Sun*, opened at Broadway's Ethel Barrymore Theater on March 11, 1959.

The cast of the original production was headlined by Sidney Poitier and consisted of other gifted actors, such as Ruby Dee and Ivan Dixon, who were then as little known as the author. That was soon corrected. The play was an instant hit, both with critics and audiences, who responded to the searing truth of Hansberry's portrayal of ordinary people whose dream of a decent life is threatened at every turn by racial and economic oppression. *A Raisin in the Sun* ran for a total of 538 performances on Broadway, an impressive tenure for a serious drama, and won the 1959 New York Drama Critics Circle Award as Best Play of the Year. Columbia Pictures quickly bought the movie rights, and the film version, with a screenplay written by Hansberry and including almost the entire original cast, made its successful debut in 1961.

*Raisin*, as it came to be called with the famil-
iarity granted to classics, made Hansberry a national
celebrity. She used her position of prominence to
emphasize the obligation of writers to involve themselves with social issues. She also supported the civil
rights movement, lending her support to such groups
as the Student Nonviolent Coordinating Committee
(SNCC). Hansberry's outspokenness antagonized a
number of whites who had expected her commercial
success to turn her into a moderate. When she criti-
cized the administration of President John F.
Kennedy for not acting vigorously enough on civil
rights, the Federal Bureau of Investigation (FBI)
began to keep a file on Hansberry, classifying her as
an ally of dangerous black militant organizations.

Hansberry privately acknowledged her homosex-
uality during the 1950s, and effectively separated
from her husband. She decided not to make her
sexual orientation public for a variety of reasons,
among them the negative reaction she anticipated
from her family and from the leadership of the
black liberation movement. Consequently, she and
Nemiroff maintained all the outward appearances of
an ongoing marriage and remained close friends,
though they lived apart. In 1963, Hansberry purchased a house in Croton-on-Hudson, just north of
New York City, and settled in to begin work on
another play.

Hansberry's new play, *The Sign in Sidney Brustein's
Window*, opened on Broadway in October 1964. The
play, which had a mostly white cast and explored

the problems confronting modern intellectuals, was a shock to many theatergoers, who had been anticipating a sequel to *A Raisin in the Sun*. The reviews were mixed, and only the dedication of Nemiroff and other supporters kept the play running for the respectable total of 101 performances.

By this time, Hansberry was facing a far graver challenge. She had begun to feel ill in 1963, and her doctors discovered that she was afflicted with cancer of the pancreas. This unpleasant news did not discourage her from writing or engaging in political activities, mainly in support of the civil rights movement in the South. In addition to completing *The Sign in Sidney Brustein's Window*, she worked on a new play entitled *Les Blancs*, which was about revolution in an African nation; a book on the English feminist Mary Wollstonecraft; and a photo essay on the civil rights movement. But there were limits to her strength. Two operations and a course of chemotherapy failed to arrest the cancer, and Hansberry's health began to decline dramatically. On January 12, 1965, she died in University Hospital in New York at the age of 34.

Neither Hansberry's work nor her influence ended with her death. She had appointed Robert Nemiroff her literary executor, and he worked diligently to realize the projects she had left unfinished. Nemiroff's stage adaptation of Hansberry's unpublished writings, *To Be Young, Gifted, and Black*, was a tremendous off-Broadway success in 1969, and *Les Blancs* was produced on Broadway the following year.

Above all, *A Raisin in the Sun* has endured as a dramatic classic. In 1974, Nemiroff produced a musical version of the play on Broadway, and the production earned the coveted Tony Award. In 1987, a new version of the original play was prepared—including the restoration of material that was previously cut—and was staged by leading theater groups throughout the nation. As long as there is an American theater, Hansberry's indictment of racism and her cry for human liberation will continue to move and enlighten audiences.

ZORA NEALE HURSTON

**O**ne of the most distinctive voices in American literature, Zora Neale Hurston was born in Eatonville, Florida, on January 7, 1891. Her parents, John and Lucy Ann, were farmers, but unlike the majority of black farmers in the United States at that time, they did not work for white land-owners. Their town, Eatonville, had been founded in 1887 to provide black Americans with a community in which they could prosper and govern themselves. The Hurstons had come to Eatonville from Alabama, bought their own land, and imbued their eight children with a sense of pride and self-worth.

As she grew up, Zora developed a forceful and independent personality that did not easily bend to discipline at home. Restless and imaginative, the young girl was equally in love with roughhousing, reading, and fantasizing. She also delighted in the local general store; whenever her parents sent her there, she eagerly soaked up all the stories, many of them deriving from African legends, that the customers swapped on the front porch. These stories were later to play an important role in her literary career.

When Zora was 13, her rich and varied life in Eatonville was ended by the death of her beloved mother. Shortly after the funeral, Zora joined two of her siblings in the city of Jacksonville, where she continued her schooling. As if it were not bad enough to be away from her cherished Eatonville, living in a city where black people were second-class citizens, Zora soon learned that her father had no intention of paying her tuition or doing anything else to support her. Returning home, she found him remarried to an attractive young woman who had no intention of being burdened with a brood of stepchildren.

Zora was sent off to live with friends of her mother's, but in fact she was alone in the world at the age of 14. For five years she wandered from place to place and from one menial job to another. Then, in 1910, Zora heard that the star of an operetta company that was touring the South needed a lady's maid. She applied for the job and was hired for what was to her the fabulous sum of $10 a week. More important, she entered a world in which her personality and her aspirations could blossom.

Hurston stayed with the operetta company until 1912, and after that there is a tantalizing gap of five years that remain a mystery to her biographers. It is known, however, that in 1917 she enrolled at the Morgan Academy, a secondary school in Baltimore. After earning her high school diploma with distinction in a single year, she became a part-time student at Howard University in Washington, D.C., where she studied English literature and embraced the ideas of W. E. B. Du Bois, who called upon black intellectuals to lead the way to a just society.

Nourishing her intellect and her flair for language at Howard, Hurston developed the ambition to become a writer. Encouraged by the publication of her first short story in the college literary magazine, she submitted a story entitled "Drenched in Light" to the New York–based magazine *Opportunity: A Journal of Negro Life*. When Charles S. Johnson, the magazine's editor, accepted the story and wrote Hurston a letter of praise, she soon decided that if she was going to succeed as a writer, she would have to move to New York.

Hurston arrived in New York in 1925 and became a full-fledged participant in the Harlem Renaissance, a remarkable flowering of African American creativity in art, literature, music, and dance. With her striking appearance, her exuberant personality, and her wealth of vivid stories about life in Eatonville, she was an instant hit with the leading lights of the Renaissance. The exhilarating atmosphere of New York stimulated Hurston's literary efforts; she won an award from *Opportunity* for her story "Drenched in Light" and contributed another story and a play to a new magazine entitled *Fire!!*

Hurston's growing literary stature also won her a scholarship to prestigious Barnard College. While majoring in English, she took a course in anthropology with the eminent scholar Franz Boas. Impressed by Hurston's intellectual abilities, Boas persuaded her to undertake a systematic study of her own heritage. When she finished her course work in 1927, Hurston traveled to the South and tried to collect folklore. She had little success in this venture, but the trip proved important for two reasons: she married her longtime boyfriend, Herbert Sheen, and struck up a friendship with the young black poet Langston Hughes.

Back in New York, Hughes introduced Hurston to Charlotte Mason, a wealthy white woman who had a keen interest in the Harlem Renaissance. The two women hit it off, and Mason offered to sponsor Hurston on another folklore-gathering trip. Hurston set off again at the end of 1927, and this time she found what she was looking for. For the next three years, Hurston visited cities and towns, farms and lumber camps, collecting stories, folktales, songs, and religious rituals. With the help of Alain Locke, who had been one of her professors at Howard, she then began to collect her material for publication.

In 1932, while working on her folklore study, *Mules and Men*, Hurston returned to Eatonville. Living in her hometown stimulated her love of storytelling, and she soon completed a story entitled "The Gilded Six-Bits." The piece was accepted by *Story*, a prestigious literary magazine, and published in 1933. Shortly afterward, Hurston received a letter from New York publisher Bertram Lippincott, praising her story and asking whether she had ever considered writing a novel. Hurston wrote back that she was indeed working on a novel; in truth, she had an idea for a novel but had not yet written a word. With typical energy she rented a little room in the nearby town of Sandford and set to work. Several months later, penniless and on the verge of eviction, she shipped the manuscript of *Jonah's Gourd Vine* off to Lippincott. To her amazement and delight, the publisher accepted her book and sent a check for $200 as an advance.

Published in 1934, *Jonah's Gourd Vine* told the story of a southern couple who were very closely modeled on Hurston's own parents. The novel was almost unanimously praised by book reviewers across the nation; *Mules and Men* appeared the following year, cementing Hurston's reputation as a serious writer and a student of black culture. She soon won a prestigious Guggenheim Fellowship and took off for the Caribbean in order to study voodoo.

Hurston conducted her research in Jamaica and in Haiti, where she claimed to have met a zombie. In addition to collecting a wealth of material on voodoo, she found time to write her second novel, *Their Eyes Were Watching God*, which was published in 1936. Relating the romantic and spiritual history of a young woman named Janie Crawford, *Their Eyes Were Watching God* endures as one of the masterworks of American literature. But its reception in the politically charged climate of 1936 was curiously mixed: white critics praised the book, but many black intellectuals attacked Hurston for writing romances instead of grappling with social problems.

Although hurt by the criticism, Hurston worked on, publishing a book on voodoo, *Tell My Horse*, in 1938. Like Janie Crawford, she also continued to search for personal fulfillment. Her marriage to Herbert Sheen had ended in 1931, and in 1939 she married a man named Albert Price III. This match proved no more satisfactory than the first, and Hurston and Price soon began to live apart, finally divorcing in 1943.

By 1940, Hurston was a nationally known writer, but she had never been able to earn a steady income from her books. Attempting to take advantage of her celebrity, she published her autobiography, *Dust Tracks on a Road*, in 1942. Her best-known work along with *Their Eyes Were Watching God*, the book got rave reviews and won her a $1,000 award from a prominent magazine. Money in hand, Hurston bought a houseboat in Daytona Beach, Florida, and settled in to continue writing. Though she sold a number of articles and another novel, she was out of money again by the end of the decade. At one point she was obliged to work as a maid, but after selling an article in 1951 she was able to rent a small house and get back to work.

Unfortunately, Hurston's ambitious new novel, *Herod the Great*, was rejected by publishers, and she continued to struggle against poverty. By 1959, suffering from a variety of ailments, she was obliged to move into a welfare home, where she died on January 28, 1960. The 69-year-old writer was buried in a segregated cemetery, in a grave that was unmarked until 1973, when writer Alice Walker discovered it and placed a headstone on it. For Hurston's epitaph, Walker chose a simple but indisputable phrase: A Genius of the South.

TONI MORRISON

One of America's literary giants, Toni Morrison was born Chloe Anthony Wofford in Lorain, Ohio, on February 18, 1931, the second of four children. Her parents, George and Ramah Wofford, had grown up in Georgia and Alabama, respectively. Their own parents had been sharecroppers, and they had vivid memories of the grinding poverty and racial intolerance endured by black people in the rural South. As a result, they took great pains to instill in their children the virtues of self-reliance and pride in their African-American heritage.

It should not be supposed, however, that the Woffords' home was a somber, joyless place to grow up. On the contrary, Toni's parents were deeply imbued with the richness of African American culture. They related many folktales and African myths to their children and stressed the importance of learning. As Morrison later recalled: "I remember myself as surrounded by extraordinary adults who were smarter than me. I was better educated, but I always thought that they had true wisdom and I had merely book learning. It was only when I began to write that I was able to marry those two things: wisdom and education."

Morrison's ability to acquire that education was a direct result of her parents' urging. They made sure that she knew how to read before she entered the first grade and encouraged all of her intellectual aspirations. In high school, Morrison devoured the classics of European literature and absorbed ideas and techniques that she would eventually put to use in her own books.

In 1949, Morrison entered Howard University in Washington, D.C., where she began calling herself "Toni," a shortened version of her middle name. Majoring in English, she expressed her flair for drama by joining the Howard Repertory Theater. Upon graduating she went on to Cornell University, where she earned a master's degree in English in 1955. After teaching for two years at Texas Southern University, she returned to Howard as a member of the faculty. For the first time she began to work seriously on her own writing and joined a group of black writers who read and discussed one another's efforts. While at Howard, she married Harold Morrison, a Jamaican-born architect. The couple had two children, Slade and Harold, but their marriage ended in divorce in 1964.

Following the breakup of her marriage, Morrison faced the challenge of supporting her two young sons alone. She soon found a job as a textbook editor with a division of Random House in Syracuse, New York. After putting in a full workday and then getting her children off to bed, she began writing late into the night. "Writing for me was the most extraordinary way of thinking and feeling," she said. "It became the one thing I was doing that I had absolutely no intention of living without." Morrison found a story she had written a few years back about a young black girl in the Midwest, Pecola Breedlove, who yearns to have blue eyes, which she considers the symbol of beauty. She turned the story into a full-length novel that explored the deep-seated effects of racism, *The Bluest Eye*. When the manuscript was completed she sent it to Holt, Rinehart & Winston, a major New York publisher. Holt agreed to publish the book, but Morrison's satisfaction was dampened by her feeling that the publishers did not really believe in her as a writer but merely wanted to capitalize on the growing interest in black literature.

Shortly after her novel was accepted, Morrison moved her family to New York City, where she began to work as a trade book editor for Random House. It was the beginning of a 16-year tenure at the publishing house, during which Morrison rose to the position of senior editor and had the opportunity to nurture and publish the work of other black writers.

Despite the demands of her job and the responsibilities of child rearing, Morrison was determined to pursue her career as a novelist. In 1973, she published her second novel, *Sula*, the tale of a young black woman determined to live by her own rules. In the book, Morrison explored the relationship between two black women—something that had rarely been attempted in American fiction. Neither *Sula* nor *The Bluest Eye* was a commercial success, but the books were well received by reviewers and established Morrison as an emerging talent.

One of Morrison's most satisfying projects at Random House was *The Black Book*, a compilation of materials on black history from the point of view of ordinary people. Acting as the coordinator of the project, Morrison helped a group of scholars and volunteers collect an array of documents and mementos from black families throughout the country. Though the resulting book was not published under her name, Morrison gained a broad and intimate view of African American life that provided powerful stimulus to her fiction.

Morrison's breakthrough into the front rank of American writers occurred in 1977 when she published her third novel, *Song of Solomon*, the story of a young African American who strives for material wealth and discovers in the process that his most valuable possession is the heritage of his people. *Song of Solomon* was hailed by critics and became a major best-seller, eventually selling 3 million copies. The novel earned Morrison the 1978 American Academy and Institute of Arts and Letters Award and also the National Book Critics' Circle Award.

Morrison's acceptance by the predominantly white, male literary elite was all the more significant in light of her racial pride and intellectual independence. As she explained to an interviewer, "My job is to not become anybody's creature, not the critical establishment's, not the media's, not anybody's. I'm not doing anyone justice, not the women's movement, not the black movement, not novels, not anyone, if I toe the line. I want to write better. Think better. I don't know how not to want that. And better for me may not be in step with what is current and prevailing."

Following the success of *Song of Solomon*, the appearance of a new novel by Morrison became a literary event. Her next work, *Tar Baby*, published in 1981, was set in the Caribbean and explored the relationship between a black woman who wants to merge herself with the affluent culture of mainstream America, and her lover, who is intent on preserving his racial and cultural identity. *Tar Baby* spent four months on the

*New York Times* best-seller list and confirmed Morrison's standing as a literary superstar.

With two best-sellers under her belt, Morrison was able to leave her job at Random House and devote herself to writing and teaching. In 1984, she was appointed to the Albert Schweitzer Chair of the Humanities at the State University of New York at Albany. While teaching courses in literature, Morrison completed her fifth novel, *Beloved*, in 1987. In this book, Morrison addressed the issue of slavery, telling the story of an escaped slave who, when caught, kills her daughter rather than have the child return to the South to grow up a slave. Hailed as both a brilliant work of fiction and a powerful exploration of American history, *Beloved* had an even greater impact than Morrison's previous books and earned her a coveted Pulitzer Prize.

In 1989, Morrison was appointed to a professorship at Princeton University, making her the first black woman to have an endowed chair at an Ivy League college. The academic environment stimulated her to write critical essays, and in 1990 she was invited to deliver the Massey Lectures in American Civilization at Harvard University; the text of these lectures was published in book form under the title *Playing in the Dark: Whiteness and the Literary Imagination*. While teaching and lecturing, Morrison continued to write fiction, and her novel *Jazz*—the exploration of a romantic triangle in 1920s Harlem—was published in 1992.

As Morrison entered her early sixties, her list of awards and honorary degrees indicated that she was not only an eminent writer but was regarded as one of the nation's cultural treasures. Her achievement is remarkable in equal measure for her creative skill and for the courage and determination that brought her gifts to fruition. If there is any single phrase that could typify Morrison as an artist, it may be this simple but far-reaching declaration: "I never played it safe in a book."

ALICE WALKER

A Pulitzer Prize–winning author and a forceful advocate of women's rights and social justice, Alice Malsenior Walker was born on February 9, 1944, in the small Georgia town of Eatonton. Alice was the eighth child of Willie Lee and Minnie Walker, sharecroppers who struggled to survive by working the land of an elderly white woman. The family's children helped work the fields and do the farm chores, but the Walkers always believed strongly in the value of education. When little Alice was four years old, her parents entrusted her to Mrs. Reynolds, the local first-grade teacher. In Reynolds's school, the young girl discovered the magic of learning and quickly proved that she had a keen intelligence.

Alice suffered a devastating blow in 1952 when she was struck in the right eye by a pellet from her brother's BB gun. Because her parents were unable to get her to a doctor right away, she lost the sight in her right eye and was disfigured by a bulbous growth of scar tissue. Previously outgoing, she now became self-conscious and withdrawn, avoiding social contact as much as possible. She lived with this burden until she was 14; at that time, while visiting one of her brothers in Boston, she consulted a doctor who removed the scar tissue. Although her right eye remained sightless, it was at least restored to its normal appearance.

Filled with renewed self-confidence, Walker returned to Eatonton and became one of the most popular students in her high school. For a time she wondered what to do with her life after graduation. That difficult question was settled one day in 1960 when she saw a civil rights demonstration led by Dr. Martin Luther King, Jr., on a television news broadcast. She understood that it was possible to struggle against the poverty and racism her own family had endured, and she vowed to dedicate her life to the cause.

When she graduated from high school in 1961, Walker entered Atlanta University's Spelman College, the nation's foremost college for black women, on a scholarship. She reveled in the study of literature, but she chafed at the conformist atmosphere of the college. Before long, however, many of Spelman's students were swept up in the battle against racial segregation, and Walker enthusiastically took part in marches and sit-ins. The crowning event of this time in her life was the March on Washington for Jobs and Freedom, which took place in the nation's capital on August 28, 1963. Perched on the limb of a tree above the crowd of 250,000 marchers, Walker heard every word of Dr. King's memorable "I Have a Dream" speech.

When the atmosphere at Spelman continued to restrict her, Walker transferred to Sarah Lawrence College in Bronxville, New York, where the study of literature awakened her interest in writing. When she graduated in 1965, Walker was committed to being an author, but she had not forgotten her devotion to civil rights. Spurning writing grants and a safer existence in New York, she returned to the South to work in voter registration drives, a project that required great physical courage in that hostile environment. While fighting segregation, she fell in love with a young law student named Mel Leventhal, and the two eventually returned to New York together.

Back in the North, Walker applied herself to her writing and published her first piece, an essay on the civil rights movement, in 1967. In the same year she married Mel Leventhal, and when he graduated from law school the couple returned to Mississippi to continue the struggle for racial justice. In 1968 Walker became writer-in-residence at Jackson State University and published her first book of poems, *Once.* The following year she published her first novel, *The Third Life of Grange Copeland,* an exploration of the lives of southern sharecroppers that revolved around a man who murdered his wife. Three days after finishing the novel, Walker gave birth to a daughter, Rebecca.

Despite her growing list of accomplishments, the pressures of work and child care—added to the hostility her interracial marriage aroused in many southerners—began to take a toll on Walker. In 1971, she accepted a short-term teaching position at Wellesley, the prestigious women's college near Boston, not realizing that she was saying good-bye to the South for good.

At Wellesley, Walker created a ground-breaking course on women writers whose work had been unjustly neglected. Her classes electrified the students who attended them and inspired Walker to produce more work of her own. In 1973, she made her first real impact on the literary scene with a book of stories, *In Love & Trouble: Stories of Black Women,* and a collection of poems, *Revolutionary Petunias & Other Poems.* Both works were praised by reviewers; the volume of stories won an award from the American Academy and Institute of Arts and Letters, and the book of poems was nominated for a National Book Award.

When Walker resettled in New York with her family in 1974, she took a job with *Ms.* magazine and continued to write. Though she soon had to cope with the death of her father and the breakup of her eight-year marriage, she worked with unflagging energy, and her second novel, *Meridian,* appeared in 1976. *Meridian,* which tells the story of a young southern woman caught up in the civil rights movement, was praised by critics and led to a Guggenheim Fellowship. Walker traveled to San Francisco in search of inspiration for a new book, and while there she fell in love with a writer and political activist named Robert Allen. When the couple settled into a cabin in northern California and were joined by Walker's daughter, a new chapter in the writer's life and career began.

Walker had been thinking about writing a historical novel for some time, and as soon as she got her bearings she threw herself into the project. The book took shape as a series of letters detailing the struggle of a young woman to overcome the brutal circumstances of her life in the rural South. Completed after a year of intensive work, *The Color Purple* was an immediate sensation. Hailed by critics as a major event in American literature, the novel captured both the 1983 American Book Award and the Pulitzer Prize. It also became a phenomenal commercial success, selling nearly 2 million copies in two years. Following up on her new status as a major author, Walker published a book of essays, *In Search of Our Mother's Gardens,* and another volume of poems, *Horses Make a Landscape Look More Beautiful.*

In 1985, director Steven Spielberg began shooting the film version of *The Color Purple*, starring Whoopi Goldberg. Walker, who had done the first draft of the screenplay, assisted the production crew on location in North Carolina, making sure that all the details of the characters' lives were accurately rendered. The film, nominated for 11 Academy Awards, not only propelled Walker's novel back onto the best-seller lists but also made her an international celebrity.

When Walker attended the film's premiere in her hometown of Eatonton, Georgia, the enthusiastic response of her former neighbors, both black and white, had long-lasting and beneficial effects. Walker's sister Ruth Walker Hood built upon the outpouring of emotion to establish The Color Purple Educational Fund Foundation, Inc., a nonprofit charitable and educational organization based in Eatonton. With Walker contributing her own time and money, the organization has, among other activities, provided scholarships to promising students in financial need.

Walker's sense of social responsibility was clearly not diluted by her newfound fame and wealth, and her creative drive was similarly undiminished. Settling back into her northern California home, Walker plunged into an ambitious new novel that attempted to retell the history of the world through the eyes of an African goddess. Published in 1989 as *The Temple of My Familiar*, the novel delighted many readers, puzzled some, and made it quite clear to everyone that Walker was a writer who would always be forging ahead and breaking new ground. Continuing her work as a poet as well, Walker collected all the poems she had written between 1965 and 1990 and published them in a single volume in 1991.

Firmly rooted in northern California, Walker has involved herself in a great variety of social and literary issues, always championing the cause of the dispossessed and neglected. In one of her essays, she eloquently described the principles that motivate her: "I have been helped, supported, encouraged, and nurtured by people of all races, creeds, colors, and dreams; and I have, to the best of my ability, returned help, support, encouragement, and nurture."

PHILLIS WHEATLEY

**P**hillis Wheatley, America's first black author, was born in 1754 on the west coast of Africa. When she was a young girl she was captured by slave traders, who shipped her to the British colonies in America to be sold. In 1761, she was unloaded from a slave ship onto Boston's Beach Street wharf, thin and frail, with nothing to cover her but a scrap of dirty carpet. In the slave market she attracted the attention of Susannah Wheatley, the wife of a Boston merchant, who was looking for a servant and was somehow drawn to the unpromising-looking girl. The merchant's wife purchased the young slave for a small sum. The seven-year-old African thus acquired a new name, derived from the family that had purchased her and from the name of the ship that had brought her to America, the *Phillis*.

Though Phillis Wheatley was now the property of another person, she was luckier than most other enslaved Africans. Of the 230,000 or so blacks in the American colonies at that time, all but about 16,000 lived in the South, where they toiled on plantations and often endured harsh treatment. In the North, the Africans were usually employed as household servants and treated with less brutality.

As she assumed her duties in the Wheatley household, young Phillis quickly showed evidence of an unusual intelligence. She grasped spoken English in a remarkably short time and soon began to read and write. Most masters, even in the North, would have been alarmed at any evidence of intellectual ambition on the part of their slaves and would have stifled it at once. But John and Susannah Wheatley were people of unusual humanity—they believed that the young girl's talents were a divine gift and that it was their duty to nourish them. Phillis later wrote of Susannah Wheatley: "I was a poor little outcast and stranger when she took me in; not only into her house, but I

presently became a sharer in her most tender affec-
tions. I was treated by her more like her child than her
servant."

At her parents' request, 18-year-old Mary Wheatley
became Phillis's tutor. Instead of working constantly,
Phillis spent several hours a day with Mary, reading
the Bible and studying poetry. By the time she was
nine years old, Phillis could read English fluently and
even understand some of the most difficult passages
in the Scriptures.

When she was 12, Phillis began to write poems.
The Wheatleys were delighted to discover this talent
in her; they provided her with all the comforts and
materials she needed and took special precautions to
protect her delicate health. At the same time, Susannah Wheatley did all she could to promote Phillis's
career as an author. She invited the leading thinkers
of Boston to converse with the young African and
sent her to the homes of prominent citizens. To the
Wheatleys' great satisfaction, Phillis proved that she
could hold her own in conversation with anyone.

Phillis quickly gained a host of admirers, including
Thomas Hutchinson, the governor of the Massachu-
setts colony, and John Hancock, who was to be a
prominent signatory of the Declaration of Independence. Nevertheless, Phillis remained a slave, and as
such she could never be accepted as an equal in white
society. Because the Wheatleys considered her far
superior to other Africans and would not allow her to
associate with members of her own race, she occupied
a peculiar—and lonely—position between two worlds.

At this time, Phillis developed a powerful religious faith, based upon the teachings of the Great Awakening, a movement that swept the colonies during the 18th century. The new doctrine was especially appealing to her because it promised salvation for all believers and held that everyone was equal in the eyes of God. Phillis embraced these beliefs with all her heart and expressed them in her poems. One of her earliest poems, written at the age of 14, was titled "An Address to the Atheist": "Thou who dost daily feel his hand, and rod/Darest thou deny the Essence of God!/If there's no heav'n, ah! whither wilt thou go . . . ?"

As Phillis Wheatley entered adolescence, the American colonists' desire for independence from Great Britain began to reach the boiling point, with occasional riots occurring over burdensome taxes imposed by the British crown. Though some colonists declared their loyalty to the mother country, Wheatley was firmly on the side of the rebellious Patriots; when British redcoats shot down five protesters in March 1770, Wheatley wrote a poem commemorating the event that became known to history as the Boston Massacre.

Wheatley achieved international notice at the age of 17 when she wrote her first major work, a poem lamenting the death of George Whitefield, a dynamic preacher who was one of the leaders of the Great Awakening. The elegy begins: "Hail, happy saint, on thine immortal throne,/Possest of glory, life and bliss unknown;/We hear no more the music of thy tongue. . . ." Published as a pamphlet and circulated among Whitefield's followers throughout the colonies and in England, the poem brought Wheatley to the attention of a wide public.

With the enthusiastic support of Susannah Wheatley, Phillis collected all the poems she had written and sought to have them published as a book. When backers could not be found in Boston, Susannah secured a publisher in England. In order to promote the project, Phillis and young Nathaniel Wheatley sailed for England in May 1773. In London, Phillis found herself an instant celebrity, but her trip was cut short after a month when news arrived that Susannah Wheatley was seriously ill. Despite Phillis's hasty departure, the publication of her book, *Poems on Various Subjects, Religious and Moral,* was a notable event. It was only the second book published by an American woman and the first by an African American.

The book received enthusiastic reviews in the British press, and not long after its publication the Wheatleys granted Phillis her freedom. She continued to live in their household, though she was now responsible for her own upkeep. In May 1774—in the midst of her deep sorrow over the death of Susannah Wheatley—Phillis finally received 300 copies of her book from London, just before the British government imposed a naval blockade on its American colonies. A year later, when redcoats and Patriots exchanged fire at Lexington and Concord, the American Revolution was under way.

Wheatley's sympathies were still fervently with the Patriots, and in 1776 she wrote a poem supporting the revolutionary cause. But the war brought her only hardship. She found it difficult to sell her books, and when John Wheatley died in 1778, he made no provision for her in his will. Perhaps as a means of survival, she married John Peters, an educated black man who ran a grocery in Boston. Wheatley appears to have lived in comfort with Peters, though she found it difficult to interest the residents of war-torn Boston in a second volume of poems.

In the early 1780s, the Peters family, which now included three children, moved from Boston to the nearby village of Wilmington. The reason for the move, apparently, was Peters's financial difficulties, and the hardships of a relatively poor life in a small village took its toll on Wheatley's health. The family moved back to Boston after the triumph of the revolution, but they did not regain their former prosperity. Records indicate that Wheatley's husband was imprisoned for debt on at least one occasion.

Despite her tribulations, Wheatley continued to write. In January 1784, she published a poetic tribute to the late Samuel Cooper, a prominent Bostonian who had been a sponsor of her first book. In September, the *Boston Magazine* carried her elegy comforting a family on the loss of a child; it was a heartfelt poem, for she had lost two of her own children. Toward the end of the year, she produced "Liberty and Peace," a poem celebrating the end of the Revolutionary War.

When "Liberty and Peace" was published, its author was unable to read it. Ill and exhausted, Phillis Wheatley had died on December 5, 1784, in a run-down boardinghouse. She was only 31 years old. No one attended her funeral, and she was buried in an unmarked grave, next to her third child, who had survived her by only a few hours. Her contemporaries did nothing to honor Phillis Wheatley, but succeeding generations have cherished her as the founder of black literature in America. There is now a monument to her in the city of Boston, honoring the remarkable woman who once wrote, "In every human breast, God has implanted a principle, which we call love of freedom; it is impatient of oppression, and pants for deliverance."

# ❧ FURTHER READING ❧

## Maya Angelou

Angelou, Maya. *I Know Why the Caged Bird Sings*. New York: Random House, 1970.

———. *Just Give Me a Cool Drink of Water 'Fore I Diiie*. New York: Random House, 1971.

Shapiro, Miles. *Maya Angelou*. New York: Chelsea House, 1994.

## Gwendolyn Brooks

Brooks, Gwendolyn. *Annie Allen*. 1949. Reprint. Westport, CT: Greenwood, 1972.

———. *Selected Poems*. New York: Harper & Row, 1963.

———. *The World of Gwendolyn Brooks*. New York: Harper & Row, 1971.

## Nikki Giovanni

Giovanni, Nikki. *Black Feeling, Black Talk*. New York: Morrow, 1970.

———. *Gemini: An Extended Autobiographical Statement on My First Twenty-five Years of Being a Black Poet*. New York: Penguin Books, 1976.

## Lorraine Hansberry

Hansberry, Lorraine. *A Raisin in the Sun*. New York: Random House, 1969.

Nemiroff, Robert, ed. *Lorraine Hansberry: The Collected Last Plays*. New York: Plume, 1983.

## Zora Neale Hurston

Hurston, Zora Neale. *Their Eyes Were Watching God*. Urbana: University of Illinois Press, 1978.

Walker, Alice, ed. *I Love Myself When I Am Laughing . . . & Then Again When I Am Looking Mean & Impressive: A Zora Neale Hurston Reader*. New York: Harcourt Brace Jovanovich, 1979.

Witcover, Paul. *Zora Neale Hurston*. New York: Chelsea House, 1991.

## Toni Morrison

Century, Douglas. *Toni Morrison*. New York: Chelsea House, 1994.

Morrison, Toni. *Beloved*. New York: Plume, 1987.

———. *Jazz*. Boston: G. K. Hall, 1993.

## Alice Walker

Gentry, Tony. *Alice Walker*. New York: Chelsea House, 1993.

Walker, Alice. *The Color Purple*. New York: Harcourt Brace Jovanovich, 1982.

———. *Possessing the Secret of Joy*. New York: Simon & Schuster, 1992.

## Phillis Wheatley

Mason, Julian D., Jr. *The Poems of Phillis Wheatley*. Chapel Hill: The University of North Carolina Press, 1966.

Richmond, Merle. *Phillis Wheatley*. New York: Chelsea House, 1988.

Shields, John, ed. *The Collected Works of Phillis Wheatley*. New York: Oxford University Press, 1988.

# ☙ INDEX ❧

# ❦ PICTURE CREDITS ❦

RICHARD RENNERT has edited the nearly 100 volumes in Chelsea House's award-winning BLACK AMERICANS OF ACHIEVEMENT series, which tells the stories of black men and women who have helped shape the course of modern history. He is also the author of several sports biographies, including *Henry Aaron*, *Jesse Owens*, and *Jackie Robinson*. He is a graduate of Haverford College in Haverford, Pennsylvania.